THIS WALKER BOOK BELONGS TO:

_____

_____

_____

_____

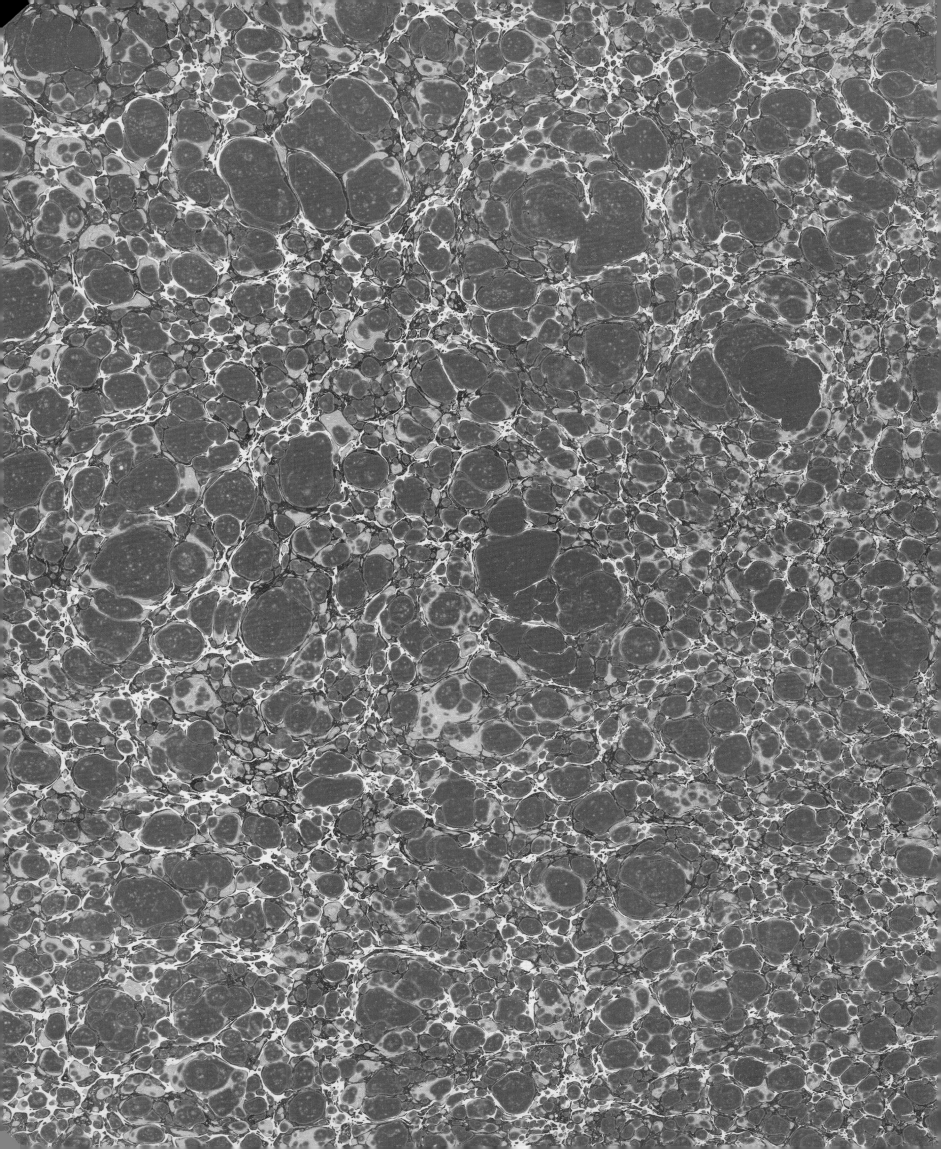

CONTENTS

Please Note, dear Reader, that within these Pages the Characters Converse in the Words which the Esteemed Mr. Dickens actually Wrote.

In you go, my friends!

For Iggy, with love

➤ *A note to readers* ➤

*When I was a child, I liked short books with lots of pictures. So, I don't think
I would ever have read Dickens, if it hadn't been for one teacher: Miss Duncan.
She was very strict, taught English and did not like fidgets! I was always a fidget –
except when she read Dickens aloud. My desk would fade from sight and I would be in
Victorian England, sharing the trials of little Oliver Twist, or shaking in my boots with Pip.
I have reread the stories many times since. The characters feel like friends to me now –
just as they did to Dickens. The tales that I have chosen to re-imagine for you here are my
five favourites. I hope that you will enjoy reading them as much
as I have enjoyed bringing them to life.*

➤ ➤

Marcia Williams

First published 2002 by Walker Books Ltd, 87 Vauxhall Walk, London SE11 5HJ

This edition published 2003 © 2002 Marcia Williams 10 9 8 7 6 5 4 3 2 1

The right of Marcia Williams to be identified as author/illustrator of this work
has been asserted by her in accordance with the Copyright, Designs and Patents Act 1988

This book has been typeset in FC Kennerley Printed in China All rights reserved

British Library Cataloguing in Publication Data:
a catalogue record for this book is available from the British Library

ISBN 0-7445-9838-9

www.walkerbooks.co.uk

CHARLES DICKENS AND FRIENDS

retold and illustrated by

Marcia Williams

WALKER BOOKS
AND SUBSIDIARIES
LONDON • BOSTON • SYDNEY

OLIVER TWIST

Let me see the child, and die.

Where she came from, or where she was going to, nobody knows.

Among other buildings in English Victorian towns, there often stood a house for the poor, known as the workhouse. On the night this story begins, a young girl collapsed in the street and was carried into one. Her shoes were worn with walking and she was heavily pregnant. The next day, in the presence of a parish doctor and a drunken nurse, she gave birth to a baby boy. Oliver breathed, sneezed and let out a cry.

It's all over, Mrs. Thingummy.

Ah, poor dear, so it is!

We name our fondlings in alphabetical order... This was a T,– Twist.

His poor mother hardly had the strength to hold him in her arms. She kissed Oliver once with her sweet, white lips, closed her eyes and died.

Her family could not be traced; nor could Oliver's father. Left a workhouse orphan, Oliver was given a surname by Mr Bumble, the parish beadle: "Twist".

The workhouse children were fed on three meals of watery gruel a day, an onion twice a week and half a roll on Sundays. They grew so hungry they used to worry they might eat each other. One evening, some of the boys cast lots to choose who would go up and ask the master for more gruel after supper. It fell to Oliver.

Oliver was nine now, but he looked much younger. His spirit was sturdy, though. Bravely, he held out his bowl to the plump, well-fed master, made his request – and got hit over the head with a ladle.

Mr Bumble marched Oliver straight before the workhouse governors. They were so horrified at his crime, they decided to get rid of him at once.

Mr Bumble put a notice on the workhouse gate, offering a reward to anyone who would take Oliver Twist off the hands of the parish.

Then he locked Oliver up in a cell. Every day he came back to beat him. Every night, Oliver shivered without a blanket and sobbed bitterly in the lonely dark. There he stayed for over a week.

Finally, Mr Sowerberry, the local undertaker, agreed to take Oliver on. Mr Bumble was delighted.

For supper, Mrs Sowerberry, a mean woman, gave Oliver scraps she'd kept by for the dog.

Then she told him to make his bed among the coffins. Oliver felt as if he were lying in a graveyard.

The next morning, he met Mr Sowerberry's assistant, Noah Claypole. Noah was a big bully.

Undertaking was a busy trade in those days. Many people died of illness or starvation. Oliver measured coffins, collected bodies and attended funerals. Noah was jealous, as Mr Sowerberry used Oliver more than him.

One day Noah went further than usual in his taunts of Oliver. He insulted his dead mother.

Meek, tiny Oliver turned into a ball of fury. He attacked Noah with all the force he could muster.

Mrs Sowerberry rushed to Noah's aid, and they pummelled and scratched Oliver.

Noah fetched Mr Bumble and Mr Sowerberry. Mr Sowerberry beat him, but Oliver would not cry.

But that night, alone among the coffins, he fell to his knees and wept.

Early next morning he packed a small bundle, slipped out into the street and set off for London.

Seven days later, Oliver limped into Barnet, just outside London, and collapsed on a step. A strange boy in huge clothes came over to talk to him.

His name was Jack Dawkins, but he liked to be called "the Artful Dodger". He said he knew a man in London who would be happy to let Oliver stay with him.

The Dodger would not enter the city till after nightfall. He led Oliver through a maze of winding streets. Even in the dark, Oliver could see and smell how filthy and wretched they were. He began to wonder whether he should run away. Then the Dodger drew him into a doorway.

They mounted some broken stairs and entered a back room. A strange old man in a ragged gown was grilling sausages at the fire. Rows of silk handkerchiefs were drying nearby. Round the table some more boys were drinking spirits and smoking long, clay pipes. The old man introduced himself to Oliver as "Fagin" and bowed deeply. Exhausted, Oliver ate a share of sausages, drank a glass of gin and hot water and fell fast asleep.

Oliver awoke next morning to find the boys gone and Fagin gloating over a box of jewels and gold.

When he realized Oliver was watching him, Fagin seized a knife and questioned him angrily.

Just then, Nancy came in. She was the girlfriend of Fagin's partner, Bill Sikes. Oliver liked her at once.

Then the Dodger came back from work. He brought more silk hand-kerchiefs and a fine, leather wallet.

Fagin, the Dodger and a boy called Charley Bates began a game that Oliver thought very funny. Fagin hid things in his pockets and the boys tried to take them out again without his noticing.

Oliver still didn't know what work the boys did, but he longed to go with them. One day he did.

The Dodger and Charley walked so slowly, Oliver feared they would be late. Then they stopped altogether by a bookstall. Suddenly, the Dodger plunged his hand into an old gentleman's pocket and ran off.

All at once Oliver realized the boys were pick-pockets. At the same moment, the old gentleman, whose name was Mr Brownlow, noticed his loss. Seeing Oliver, he began to run after him. Soon everyone in the street had left their business and joined in the chase. Oliver was caught and taken before the magistrate.

Mr Fang, the magistrate, a stern man, thought Oliver deserved three months' hard labour.

But then the bookstall owner arrived and told the true story. Mr Fang discharged Oliver.

A few moments later Mr Brownlow passed him in the street, shivering from fever and shock.

The old gentleman felt very sorry for Oliver. He lifted him into his arms and took him home.

Oliver was ill for weeks. Mrs Bedwin, Mr Brownlow's house-keeper, nursed him tenderly.

Above his head hung a portrait of a young woman. Mr Brownlow was struck by how like her Oliver looked.

Oliver had never known so much kindness. As he got better, he grew anxious to repay it.

So when Mr Brownlow asked him to return some books and money for him, he rushed off at once.

As he left, Mr Grimwig arrived for tea. Mr Grimwig was very fond of muffins.

But he was not very fond of boys. He jeered at Mr Brownlow for trusting Oliver with money.

But Mr Brownlow had absolute faith in Oliver. He was sure he would be back in twenty minutes.

The two friends sat down to wait. Twenty minutes passed. An hour. It got dark, but Oliver did not return.

The morning that the Dodger and Charley Bates came home without Oliver, Fagin had been furious.

He sent Bill Sikes and Nancy to keep watch on Mr Brownlow's house. Nancy did not want to go.

But Bill and Fagin made her. As Oliver set off on his errand, she and Bill grabbed him by the arms.

Back at Fagin's, Mr Brownlow's money and Oliver's new clothes were taken from him. Fagin wanted to beat him, but Nancy snatched the club away.

Oliver was kept prisoner for over a week, without light or company. Then, one night, Nancy fetched him. He was to go to the country on a job with Bill.

Next morning they started. They walked all day and half the night. At last they reached a lonely house. Oliver realized Bill was going to burgle it.

Oliver tried to run away, but Bill lifted him up to a small window. He put a lantern in his hand, pushed him through and trained his pistol on him.

Oliver had just decided to wake the family instead of letting Bill in, when he heard a loud noise and felt a pain in his arm. A servant had shot him.

Bill leaned in, dragged Oliver out and ran. But the servants gave chase. Bill dumped Oliver's bleeding body into a ditch and made his escape.

Vice ... takes up her abode in many temples.

But even if he has been wicked, think how young he is.

My dear love ... do you think I would harm a hair of his head?

To Oliver's amazement, he woke up in a warm, comfortable bed. Beside him sat an old woman called Mrs Maylie and a young one called Rose. The bed and the ladies were all in the house Bill Sikes had planned to rob. Instead of calling a constable when they found Oliver, the women had called a doctor.

If they knew how happy I am, they would be pleased.

I am sure they would.

Mrs Maylie and Rose believed Oliver's story and took great care of him. Once his arm was healed, Rose promised to take him to London to see Mr Brownlow.

How do you feel tonight, Bill?

As weak as water ... let me get off this thundering bed anyhow.

Meanwhile, in London, Bill had been ill since the failed burglary. Nancy nursed him devotedly, but she, Bill and Bull's-eye, Bill's dog, were thin and hungry.

One night Nancy went to borrow money from Fagin. While she was there, a man called Monks visited. Nancy listened in wonder at the words she overheard.

I have stolen away from those who would surely murder me...

It wrings my heart to hear you!

The next evening, she gave Bill a sleeping draught and went out. She walked to a hotel she had heard Monks mention. Rose Maylie and Oliver were staying there.

Do you know a man named Monks? ... He knows you; and knew you were here.

I never heard the name.

Nancy told Rose that Monks was Oliver's half-brother. Their father had left money to Oliver, provided he did no wrong. Monks was paying Fagin to recapture Oliver and turn him into a thief so that he would not inherit.

I pity you!

I am drawn back to him through every suffering and ill-usage.

Nancy had risked her life to come. Rose begged her to stay, but Nancy loved Bill.

13

Next day, Rose took Oliver to meet Mr Brownlow and Mrs Bedwin. Trusting Mr Brownlow at once, Rose decided to confide Nancy's story to him.

Mr Brownlow was determined to track down Monks. Nancy had promised to walk on London Bridge each Sunday at midnight. They went together to meet her.

They followed Nancy down some steps. She whispered a description of Monks and named a pub he often drank at. Suddenly Mr Brownlow realised he knew the man. What none of them guessed was that the suspicious Fagin had sent Noah Claypole, Oliver's old tormentor, to spy on them. He had heard every word.

When Noah told Fagin that Nancy had betrayed Monks, he fell into a foul rage. He made Noah repeat his story to Bill. Before the boy could finish, Bill rushed home, pulled Nancy from her bed and killed her.

But it was too late. Mr Brownlow knew how to find Monks and he did so at once. He was right, he did know the man. Monks' father, Edwin Leeford, had been his oldest friend. Leeford had been unhappily married to Monks' mother. Before he died, Edwin had given Mr Brownlow a portrait of the woman he truly loved: Agnes Fleming. It was this picture that had so startled Mr Brownlow with its likeness to Oliver.

After Nancy's death, Fagin was arrested, and the boys and Bill went into hiding in a ruined house. One night, a suspicious crowd gathered outside it. Bill tied a rope round the chimney, intending to jump to the ground and escape. But, as he slipped it over his head, he imagined he saw Nancy's dying face and lost his footing. The noose tightened round his neck and he swung lifeless. Bull's-eye jumped after him – and died too.

And now this story is almost ended. Oliver was to see Fagin once more – in prison. He and Mr Brownlow went to ask him about some of Monks' papers. The old man had lost his wits. Meek and enraged by turns, he took Oliver by the shoulders and tried to escape with him. The guard pulled him back, but his shrieks followed them out of the prison and past the gallows where he was to be hanged the next morning.

Mr Brownlow adopted Oliver and moved with Mrs Bedwin to the country, close to Rose and Mrs Maylie. A stone was set in the churchyard in memory of Agnes Fleming. Whenever he can, Mr Grimwig visits them on Sundays to fish and eat muffins. Mr Brownlow often reminds him of how wrong he was to say Oliver would not come back. And often, Mr Grimwig promises to eat his head. But he never has yet!

GREAT EXPECTATIONS

AS TOLD BY PHILIP PIRRIP
THAT CAME TO BE
CALLED PIP

A.Q.
SLEEP IN HEAVENLY PEACE

P.P.
AT REST

Pray don't do it, sir.

ALSO GEORGIANA

R.I.P.

One Christmas Eve, when I was seven, I walked out to the churchyard on the marsh, to visit my parents' graves. I was an orphan, and lived with my sister and her husband Joe, the blacksmith. Suddenly, a man rose out of the mist and grabbed me. He wore an iron ring round his ankle, so I knew he was an escaped convict. Learning I lived at the forge, he made me promise to bring him food and a file next morning – or be killed. He warned me not to tell a soul, or his friend, hidden in the fog, would tear out my heart and liver.

You're a foul shrew.

Mrs. Joe has been out a dozen times, looking for you, Pip.

Where have you been, you young monkey?

Drat that boy.

You come along and be dosed.

You're a foul shrew.

Terrified, I fled home. Joe met me and warned me that my sister was "on the rampage" as I was late. She had a vile temper and a cane that Joe called "Tickler".

I hid but she soon found me. She whacked me with "Tickler". Then she dosed Joe and I with tar-water – disgusting stuff she said would do us good.

Holloa, young thief!

What larks!

I slept little and rose early. From the pantry I stole bread, cheese, mincemeat and a whole pork pie.

I poured brandy from a bottle and refilled it with what I took to be water from a nearby jug.

I fetched a file and ran. I don't know who I was more scared of, my sister or my convict's friend.

I think you have got the ague.

Where is he? ... I'll pull him down, like a bloodhound.

In the mist I thought I saw my convict asleep. But it was the man who took out hearts and livers!

When I did find my convict he was shivering and hungry. As he ate, I felt very sorry for him.

I told him I had seen his friend, but to my surprise he grew angry. I felt afraid of him and slipped away.

Have a little brandy, uncle.

TAR!

We had guests for Christmas dinner. All through the meal, I sat wretched with worry that my sister would find out my theft. I thought I was lost when she poured Joe's uncle some of the watered-down brandy. I was amazed when he leapt to his feet, whooping and coughing. I had refilled the brandy bottle with tar-water!

Let us have a cut.

You must taste ... a savoury pork pie.

Gracious goodness gracious me, what's gone - with - the - pie!

I am on a chase in the name of the King.

My sister was mystified, but suggested she fetch a lovely pork pie she had in the pantry. Knowing she wouldn't find it there, I got up and ran.

I got no further than the door, where I met a party of soldiers. Luckily, they had not come to arrest me, but wanted help searching for two escaped convicts.

Pip, old chap! ... What larks!

He tried to murder me.

Surrender, you two!

I took some wittles, up at the willage over yonder...

Stole.

We wouldn't have you starved to death... Would us, Pip?

Joe suggested he and I join in the search. The marsh was as misty as ever, but we soon heard the men. They were fighting noisily.

I was worried my convict might think I'd brought the soldiers. But when he "confessed" to stealing food from the local forge, I knew he didn't blame me.

Why, how ever could Tar come there?

Tar!

Poor miserable fellow-creatur.

What larks!

Would us, Pip?

The following winter, I was invited to Satis House, the home of a rich old spinster called Miss Havisham. Miss Havisham had been jilted on her wedding day.

She still wore her ragged wedding gown. I was to play with her adopted daughter, Estella. I thought Estella very pretty, but she thought me common.

Even so, six days later I was invited again. This time I helped Miss Havisham walk around a great table. It was laden with her mouldering wedding feast. I learnt that Miss Havisham's life had stopped on her wedding morning. The sun had not entered her windows since, nor the clocks ticked. And in revenge for her broken heart, Estella must be brought up to break the hearts of men.

After our walk, Estella and I played cards. Miss Havisham kept asking me if I found Estella pretty.

As I left, I met a pale-faced boy who wanted to fight me. Estella seemed very pleased when I won.

But then she put a plate of food before me on the ground. I felt like a dog in disgrace and wept.

Although she was so cruel, Estella fascinated me. I told my good friend, Biddy, all about her. I said I wished I were a gentleman fit to marry her.

The more often I visited Satis House, the more I despised my humble home. I tried to educate myself and Joe so we would not be "common".

One day, Miss Havisham noticed I was taller and dismissed me. As a reward for my visits, she gave Joe money to pay for me to become his apprentice.

I hated being a blacksmith. I poured out my discontent to Biddy and talked to her endlessly on my favourite subject: Estella.

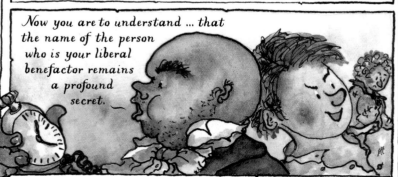

Four long years passed. Then one night a London lawyer, Mr Jaggers, came to tell Joe and I that I was rich. I had a secret patron and great expectations.

I was sure my patron was Miss Havisham. She wanted me to be educated as a gentleman and then marry Estella. I left my old home without regret.

THIS IS THE END OF THE FIRST STAGE OF PIP'S EXPECTATIONS

Pray come in.

TRY BARNARD'S MIXTURE.

Sulk

In London, I shared lodgings with the pale-faced fighter I had met at Satis House, Herbert Pocket.

We were soon good friends. He corrected my country manners in such a friendly way, I didn't mind.

His father, Matthew, was my tutor. He taught one other boy – an idle brute called Bentley Drummle.

The months passed and I never returned home to visit Joe. One day Estella wrote to say she was going to stay in London. I went to meet her off the coach. She was more beautiful than I had ever seen her.

Not long after, I met her at a ball. I was upset to see that she let Bentley Drummle hang about her.

So proud ... and so inflexible.

Estella won many admirers in London. But although I haunted picnics, concerts, parties and plays just to catch a glimpse of her, she only ever treated me as her younger brother or poor relation.

Herbert and I began to run up debts. We were young and money seemed easier to spend than save.

They are mounting up.

One evening, as Herbert and I pretended to do our accounts, a letter with a black seal came for me. It told me my sister had died. There were no excuses now. I went home for the funeral and to see Joe and Biddy.

Back in London I soon forgot my intentions to visit Joe more often. The months rolled into years and all Herbert and I could show for them were bigger debts.

My twenty-first birthday came round. Herbert and I were sure I would learn my patron's identity then. But Mr Jaggers would still give nothing away.

Then, one winter's night, I heard a heavy tread on the stair. I took up my lamp and went out.

A filthy, weatherbeaten man held out his hands to me. I recoiled in horror, yet I knew him. In a flash, I stood in a misty churchyard, seven years old again. He was my convict! "Abel Magwitch", as he told me now.

Magwitch told me that after we last met, he had been sent to Australia. To repay my childhood kindness, he had worked for the money to make me a gentleman.

A convict was my patron! I could not believe it. One thing was certain – I must earn my own living now and not take another penny from him.

I asked Magwitch about the man who tore out livers. Compeyson was his old enemy, he said; a villain who had once swindled an heiress by jilting her at the altar.

That night I did not sleep. My expectations were all in ashes. Miss Havisham had never planned that I should marry Estella. I had deserted Joe for a mere dream.

THIS IS THE END OF THE SECOND STAGE OF PIP'S EXPECTATIONS

I'm a heavy grubber, dear boy.

What is to be done?

~ The first and main thing to be done, is to get him out of England.

Herbert joined us at breakfast. Magwitch told us he would hang if he was found on English soil.
Herbert suggested we make plans to row downriver and try to board one of the Rotterdam steamers.

I have loved you long and dearly.

You address nothing in my breast.

Before we left, I went to declare my love for Estella and tell her I no longer had great expectations.
She told me she was engaged to Bentley Drummle.

I stole her heart away and put ice in its place.

Better ... to have left her a natural heart, even to be bruised or broken.

I was distraught. I went to Miss Havisham and told her that her bitterness had ruined two young lives.
She had frozen Estella's heart and broken mine.

I had never seen Miss Havisham shed a tear, but now she wept. As I turned to go, a light sprang from the fire and her wedding rags burst into flame. I threw the tablecloth over her and wrestled her to the ground.
We were both badly burnt, but Miss Havisham never recovered her mind, and not long afterwards she died.

Compeyson.

I apprehend that man...

The night Herbert and I chose for Magwitch's escape, another boat pulled alongside. Compeyson had traced Magwitch, followed us and informed the law.

And I love her!

Magwitch was sentenced to hang. But in prison he fell ill. As I nursed him, I came to love him. Before he died, I told him I'd learnt Estella was his daughter.

After Magwitch died I tried to sort out my debts. But I had no money and faced prison. Herbert had gone abroad to work. I fell ill with loneliness and worry.

One morning my fever cooled and I woke to see a familiar shape by my bedside. Dear, good Joe had paid off my debts and come to nurse me.

I was full of sorrow for the years of wrong I had done Joe. When I was well again, I followed him home to ask his forgiveness. I also hoped that Biddy might marry me. To my amazement, I found it was Joe and Biddy's wedding morning! It seemed I was fated to live my life alone. I left England and went to work for Herbert.

It was eleven years before I saw Joe and Biddy again. One December evening, just after dark, I lifted the latch of the old kitchen door. By the glow of the fire, I saw not just my two dear friends, but two beautiful children as well. One was a boy, named "Pip" after me.

The next evening, I walked to the site of Satis House. In the misty starlight, I saw a figure – Estella. Her face told me she had suffered much. I had heard how cruel Drummle had been to her, but also that he had lately died. I took her hand and led her away from that ruined place.

THE END

A TALE OF TWO CITIES

Recalled to Life

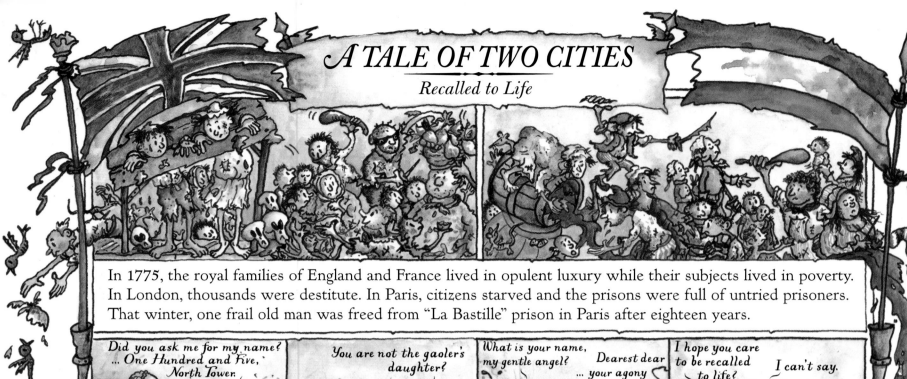

In 1775, the royal families of England and France lived in opulent luxury while their subjects lived in poverty. In London, thousands were destitute. In Paris, citizens starved and the prisons were full of untried prisoners. That winter, one frail old man was freed from "La Bastille" prison in Paris after eighteen years.

His name was Doctor Manette. Long ago, he had seen a peasant girl and boy killed by the cruel Marquis of Evrémonde and his brother. To ensure his silence, they had thrown him in gaol without trial. Now, weak and bewildered, the doctor was travelling to London with his old friend, Mr Lorry, and his daughter, Lucie.

The doctor noticed little of what went on around him but kept busy at his prison work of shoemaking. He could not remember his name, only his cell number.

The Channel crossing was rough, but with the help of Charles Darnay, a fellow passenger, Lucie settled her father comfortably and at last he slept.

In London, the Manettes took rooms in Soho and Miss Pross, who had looked after Lucie since her mother's death, came to live with them. Mr Lorry often visited. Surrounded by their warmth and far from the shadow of La Bastille, Doctor Manette began to recover. He even took up being a doctor again.

But Doctor Manette kept his shoemaking bench. And though he was devoted to Lucie, he never spoke to her of his time in prison, or why he'd been there.

Then Charles Darnay was tried at the Old Bailey as a French spy. Because they had crossed the Channel with him, the Manettes were called as witnesses.

Poor Charles. From the dock he saw that every face in the crowded courtroom believed him guilty.

Except one. As he denied the charges put to him, his eyes met Lucie's compassionate gaze.

When she was called to the witness box, Lucie spoke eloquently of Charles' kindness to her father. But her words were not enough to save him.

While the next witness was called, a rumpled-looking lawyer called Sydney Carton tossed a note to Mr Stryver, who was defending Charles.

Mr Stryver asked the new witness to be sure he had correctly identified the prisoner. Then he asked Sydney to take off his wig and stand beside Charles.

The crowd gasped. Though Sydney was scruffy and Charles neat, they could have been twins. To Lucie's relief, the case collapsed. Charles went free.

25

I have sometimes ... made the echoes out to be the echoes of all the foot-steps that are coming by-and-by into our lives.

There is a great crowd coming ... if that be so.

After the trial, Sydney and Charles often walked over to the Manettes'. Lucie imagined she heard other footsteps coming too, of people she had yet to meet.

Sydney was silent and moody and Lucie felt shy with him. She felt easier with Charles. He was modest, charming and always cheerful.

If ever there were love in the world, I love her.

One morning, when Lucie was out, Charles told her father that he was in love with Lucie. He said that if ever they married, he must tell the doctor something.

Think now and then that there is a man who would give his life, to keep a life you love beside you!

Sydney loved Lucie too. One day he spoke to her passionately. He said he knew she did not return his love, but he would give up his life for her happiness.

Indeed?

I am very much put out about my Ladybird.

Miss Pross grew quite crotchety about all the new visitors coming to the house. But she was happy too when her "Ladybird" and Charles got engaged.

On his wedding morning, Charles told the doctor his real name was not Darnay but "Evrémonde". His family – all dead now – had been French aristocrats.

When the doctor realized that the men who'd gaoled him had been his new son-in-law's uncle and father, a fit of madness overcame him.

It is such an old companion.

I am sure it does no good.

After nine days, he recovered. He let Mr Lorry burn his shoemaker's bench. Time passed, and peace and a grandchild, "little Lucie", blessed the household.

Across the Channel in Paris, there was little peace. The hatred the poor felt for the rich had turned to violent revolution. On July the fourteenth, 1789, Monsieur and Madame Defarge, who owned a wine-shop in a poor quarter of the city, handed out arms and joined an angry crowd heading for La Bastille. They stormed the prison and freed the prisoners. In one cell – One Hundred and Five, North Tower – Monsieur Defarge found a written paper. He stuffed it in his pocket and went on.

The revolutionaries seized control of Paris and gaoled hundreds of aristocrats and their servants. Charles Darnay rode to Paris. He had come to plead for the life of an old family servant.

At the city gate, Monsieur Defarge read the name "Evrémonde" on Charles' papers and led him straight to La Force prison. He refused Charles' request to send word to Mr Lorry, who was working in Paris.

Thank God, that no one near and dear to me is in this dreadful town to-night.

A few nights later, as Mr Lorry worked late in his Paris offices, he was startled to hear the bell sound at the gate.

What has happened?

My husband! ... He was stopped at the barrier, and sent to prison.

I have a charmed life in this city. I have been a Bastille prisoner.

He was even more startled to see Doctor Manette, Lucie, "little Lucie" and Miss Pross. When he heard Charles was held at La Force, he looked very grave and led the doctor to the window.

If you really have the power you think you have ... make yourself known to these devils, and get taken to La Force.

Below, a crowd of drunken citizens were sharpening their knives at a huge grindstone. They were going to the prisons to kill aristocrats. Doctor Manette raced downstairs.

Live the Bastille prisoner!

Save the prisoner Evrémonde!

He told the crowd of his own unjust imprisonment and was greeted as a hero. For his sake, they spared Charles' life.

Be merciful to my husband.

Is it likely...?

But the next day, Lucie met Madame Defarge. Her pleas for Charles' safety fell on deaf ears.

I know that I can save him, Lucie.

Only the doctor was allowed to visit La Force. He brought news that Charles was well.

But Lucie still worried. Whenever she saw Madame Defarge, she shivered with foreboding.

Take off his head!

A citizeness of France?

Daughter of ... the good physician.

At last, the day of Charles' trial came. When the tribunal heard that Doctor Manette was his father-in-law, they forgave him his birth and set him free.

He is denounced ... by the Citizen and Citizeness Defarge.

And by one other.

Denounce

But that night there came a knock at the Manettes' door and Charles was rearrested. He must stand trial for his life, for the third time, in the morning.

The Final Trial

The next day, Monsieur Defarge gave the court the paper he had found at La Bastille. Written in the doctor's hand, it told the true story of his imprisonment – the story Lucie and Charles had never heard. He had written it in his cell in case he died there. After it was read out, Madame Defarge spoke. The children killed by Charles' father and uncle had been her brother and sister. Lucie was overcome with grief. There was no hope for Charles. He must mount the guillotine and pay the price for his family's crime.

But Sydney had heard of Charles' danger and come to Paris to see if he could help. That night, he visited his cell, drugged him and changed clothes with him.

An accomplice took Charles to a waiting coach in which Mr Lorry and the Manettes were to travel back to London. Mr Lorry had Sydney's papers.

Next day, while Charles rode out of France, Sydney rode to the scaffold. His thoughts were of Lucie; his face was radiant and calm. Only the young seamstress beside him recognized him. He held her hand to comfort her. As the blade of the guillotine rose and fell, she died. As it rose and fell again, Sydney died also.

The PERSONAL HISTORY of David Copperfield

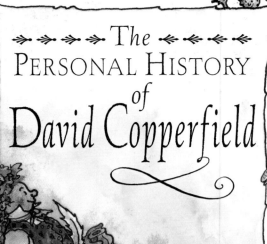

I beg you'll call her Betsey Trotwood.

Ma'am, I am happy to congratulate you.

Ba-a-ah! Ya-a-ah!

Before I was born, my father's aunt came from Dover to visit my mother. She was sure I would be a girl.

When the doctor came to tell her that I was a boy, she vanished like a discontented fairy!

Cock-a-doodle-doo!

Davy?

Master Davy!

VACANCY

My pretty mother, Clara, named me David Copperfield after my late father. She missed my father but was delighted with her new son.

She, my good nurse Peggotty and I lived together at The Rookery. We were excellent friends and my early years were very happy.

Pretty little widow.

~ Bewitching.

~ Shake hands!

Oh Davy!

It wo~ ~ do.

Then Mr Murdstone came to darken our lives. He was stern and handsome. He began to court my mother and she was too gentle to resist him. I didn't like his ill-omened black eyes and I don't think Peggotty did either.

Barkis is willin'.

You'll find us rough, sir, but you'll find us ready.

One day, Peggotty invited me to stay with her brother by the sea. Mr Barkis, who drove us, took quite a shine to Peggotty. When we arrived, I saw that Mr Peggotty's house was a boat! I also found that I would have a friend to play with: his niece, little Em'ly. I loved her at once and she loved me. The days flew by.

Ba-a-ah!

Ba-a-ah!

Not such a one as this, Mr. Copperfield wouldn't have liked.

Sweet hearts.

But when I went home I found Mr Murdstone had married my mother.

Everything was changed. My dear old bedroom had been moved.

The empty kennel was filled with Mr Murdstone's snarling dog.

Then Mr Murdstone's sister came to stay. She took my mother's keys and began to run the household.

Mr and Miss Murdstone also took charge of my education. They made me too nervous to learn.

One morning, Mr Murdstone held a cane. Whole pages of my lessons slipped away from me.

Grimly, Mr Murdstone walked me to my room. He held my head in a vice and prepared to beat me.

In a panic, I caught his hand and bit it through. He beat me then as if he would beat me to death.

Then he was gone and my door was locked. I felt sore and sad and very wicked.

For five days I remained a prisoner. I saw no one but Miss Murdstone. I might have gone mad had I not found my father's old books to read.

On the fifth night I heard Peggotty whispering at the door. She said I was to be sent to school. She slipped me two half-crowns, wrapped with my mother's love.

Salem House School

I hate old Creaky

My first School

SILENCE

Bow, wow, wow, Whose dog art thou?

NO SMILING NO LAUGHING BY ORDER

Towser! Fetch! Good dog!

I'M A TARTAR.

You won't rub the marks out that I shall give you.

Mr Barkis took me to my new school. When I arrived, a placard was fixed to my back to warn people that I was a biter. I felt like a dog.

Mr Creakle was our headmaster. He never spoke above a hoarse whisper and loved to slash us with a cane. My placard got in his way, so he tore it off.

NO TALKING

BLESS THIS HOUSE

Whisper, whisper.

Aaaagh! I'll take care of you.

You're very kind ... I am very much obliged to you.

We'll make some regular Arabian Nights of it.

There was only one boy Mr Creakle did not cane, James Steerforth. He was older than the rest of us and extremely handsome. He was my hero. He kindly took the money my mother had given me and spent it on a dormitory feast.

He also kindly asked me to tell him the stories in my father's old books.

SUNDAY STAY INDOORS NO PLAYING

She's getting to be a woman.

When I say I will have a thing done, I will have it done.

I have something to tell you, my child.

Once Mr Peggotty visited me with news of little Em'ly. He invited Steerforth and I to his boat home.

The days dragged by in a blur of cracked slates, canings and tear-blotted copybooks.

Then, on my birthday, Mrs Creakle told me I must go home. My dear pretty mother had died.

I'm a Tartar.

I broke into a desolate cry. I was an orphan. All day I cried and slept and cried again.

And so I left Salem House. I had not been happy there, but I dreaded seeing the Murdstones again.

After my mother's funeral, Peggotty married her suitor, Mr Barkis. The Murdstones didn't know what to do with me. Eventually, they sent me to London, to earn my living in the wine trade. My job was to paste labels on the bottles, cork, seal and pack them. I was only ten years old. My tears mingled with the warehouse filth.

I lodged at the home of the Micawber family. They were my only friends. Mr Micawber was wonderful with words but not so wonderful with money.

He was always in debt and eventually the family was taken away to prison. I visited them there every day and shared my meagre earnings with them.

But then, happily, they were released. They decided to make a fresh start in Plymouth. I would be alone again. As I waved them off, I made a brave resolution. I would run away from my job and make my way to Dover, to find my only living relation: Miss Betsey Trotwood.

I arrived in Dover footsore and ragged. My aunt was outside, guarding her lawn from donkeys.

When I told her who I was, she flopped down on the grass and stared at me until I started to cry.

At that, she took me indoors to meet her friend, Mr Dick, who was very fond of kites.

After a few days of rest and good food, I began to feel very much at home with my aunt and Mr Dick.

I was terrified when the Murdstones arrived to take me back. But I need not have been. After only a short meeting my aunt sent them packing!

She and Mr Dick became my guardians. I was very happy. I had a new life, new clothes and a new name, Trotwood Copperfield, or "Trot" for short.

My aunt and I decided I should go to school in nearby Canterbury. During the week I would board with Mr Wickfield, her lawyer, and his daughter, Agnes.

Agnes kept house for her father, as her mother had died. She was very kind and wise, and soon became as dear to me as a sister.

My new school was not like Salem House. There were no canes. I studied hard and played hard.

The years flew by. As I grew, I fell in and out of love. I confided each of my passions to Agnes.

My only unease was with Uriah Heep, Mr Wickfield's fawning assistant. He was a schemer.

Heep gained control over Mr Wickfield, who began to drink, and then made Heep his partner.

By a strange twist of fate, Heep employed my old friend, Mr Micawber, as his clerk.

Worst of all, Heep told me that he planned to marry Agnes some day. When the time came for me to leave school, my aunt expressed a wish that I should train as a lawyer in London. The thought of leaving sweet Agnes behind in the same house as the awful Heep was almost unbearable.

My aunt paid for me to be apprenticed to a London lawyer, Mr Spenlow. But my heart was not in the work. I found it dry and dusty.

One Sunday Mr Spenlow invited me to meet his daughter, Dora. I fell in love with her in an instant. She was so sweet. Though Jip, her dog, was not.

I wanted to marry Dora at once. But one evening I returned to my lodgings to find my aunt Betsey, Mr Dick, a cat, two birds and a pile of luggage. My aunt was bankrupt. She and Mr Dick had moved to London.

To earn some money for us all, I tried my hand at writing. Soon I was selling my stories!

Eventually I made enough money to marry Dora. I loved my little wife and our marriage started happily. But we were young and very bad at housekeeping. To my mind, Dora was not serious enough. She liked playing with Jip and strumming her guitar. Sometimes I wished that she were more like Agnes.

But once I learnt to accept her just as she was, we were happy. But then Dora miscarried our baby. She grew ill and weak and had to stay in bed.

One day we were surprised by an urgent summons to Canterbury from Mr Micawber. I was loath to leave Dora, but she insisted I accompany my aunt.

I Return to Canterbury to Assist at an Explosion!

When we arrived we were met by a tense Mr Micawber.

Madam ... I trust you will shortly witness an eruption.

He ushered us into the office of the humble and fawning Heep.

An unexpected pleasure!

After the Wickfields joined us, Mr Micawber exploded.

If there is a scoundrel on this earth ... that scoundrel's name is – HEEP!

Mr. W. has been for years deluded and plundered, in every conceivable manner, to the pecuniary aggrandisement of the avaricious, false, and grasping – HEEP.

As his clerk, Mr Micawber had discovered all the ways in which Uriah Heep had tricked Mr Wickfield over the years.

My services were constantly called ... for the falsification of business.

Micawber, you old bully.

He had also swindled many of Mr Wickfield's clients out of their wealth – including my aunt. She was furious and shook Heep by the collar.

You know what I want?

A strait-waistcoat.

We demanded that Heep pay back every farthing he had stolen. Otherwise we would inform the law. After an angry outburst, Heep agreed.

Copperfield, I have always hated you ....you've always been against me.

It is you who have been, in your greed and cunning, against all the world.

Mr Micawber was quite the hero! Her wealth restored, my aunt offered to pay for his family's passage to Australia. He was delighted at the idea.

I wonder you have never turned your thoughts to emigration.

It was the dream of my youth.

I never will desert him!

Agnes

Back in London, Dora grew weaker. Agnes came to visit her, but that night Dora and Jip both died. I was heartbroken. Then I heard that my old hero, Steerforth, had lured away Mr Peggotty's niece, little Em'ly, with false promises of marriage. Filled with these sorrows, I went abroad and stayed away for three years.

In that time I came to understand many things, especially how much Agnes meant to me. She wrote often, but I missed her terribly. I decided to return to find out if she loved me. My aunt and Mr Dick had moved back to Dover. Peggotty, a widow now, lived with them. We were all four delighted to see one another again!

My aunt and I talked far into the night. My aunt hinted that Agnes had plans to marry. I decided to ride over and visit her in the morning.

It was wonderful to see Agnes again. Over the next weeks, I visited her often. But she never did confide her marriage plans to me.

Eventually, I could keep my secret no longer. I told Agnes how much I loved her. To my amazement, I found she had a secret too. She loved me! To everyone's delight we were soon married.

A Last Retrospect

Agnes told me that before Dora died, she had confided her hope that Agnes and I might marry one day. Dear Dora, she knew me better than I knew myself. Long happy years have passed since then. Mr Micawber is doing well in Australia. So is Mr Peggotty, who emigrated with little Em'ly. I have my friends and family close about me. Mr Dick plays with our boys and keeps Agnes' father company. My aunt spoils our little daughter, named Betsey Trotwood after her. My old nurse, Peggotty, wears stronger spectacles, but still cares for us all. And always by my side is Agnes – steadfast and true. I have her love to guide me through the years to come.

THE END

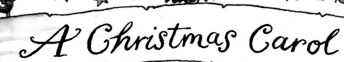

A Christmas Carol

Everyone knew old Ebenezer Scrooge was the most tight-fisted miser you could meet. His business partner, Jacob Marley, dead these seven years, had been the same. One Christmas Eve, Scrooge sat in his cold office counting the coals Bob Cratchit, his clerk, put on the fires. He grumbled that Christmas was all "humbug".

When Fred, his nephew, burst in to invite him for Christmas dinner, Scrooge crossly refused.

When two gentlemen came collecting money for the poor, he sent them away empty-handed.

When a little boy started to sing a carol through the keyhole, Scrooge took a ruler to him.

The cold day turned to bitter night and Scrooge let Bob go home at last. He did not wish him a Merry Christmas, just begrudged him the next day off.

You will not be surprised to hear that Scrooge's tavern meal that night was meagre. Nor that the lodgings he made his way to afterwards were lonely.

But you may be surprised to learn what he saw when he got there. Marley's face was in the knocker.

It was in the fireplace tiles too. Then all the bells began to ring and a chain clanked upon the stair.

Yet even when old Marley floated through the door, Scrooge did not believe these things. He told the ghost he was the product of his undigested supper.

At this, the ghost untied the bandage round his head and as his jaw fell to his chest, a fearful wail came out of it. Scrooge fell quaking to his knees.

Marley told Scrooge the chain of keys and cash-boxes he wore had been forged during his miserly life. He warned Scrooge to change his ways before he died or he would become a fettered phantom too.

Three more ghosts would visit Scrooge tonight. Marley warned him to learn from them.

Then, as Scrooge stared, the window opened itself and old Marley's ghost floated backwards out of it. The night air he joined was thick with moaning phantoms. Each one wore a heavy chain.

Still in his dressing-gown, Scrooge fell into bed. He tried to say "humbug", but couldn't.

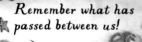

The Ghost of Christmas Past

Scrooge slept fitfully. When the clock struck, a ghostly hand parted his bed curtains.

I am the Ghost of Christmas Past.

A jet of light shone out of the Ghost's head. Under its arm, it held its hat: a giant candle-snuffer.

I am mortal ... and liable to fall.

Gently, it took the bewildered Scrooge by the arm and guided him back through the years.

Poor boy!

HAPPY CHRISTMAS

$4 \times \frac{1}{2} = 2$

$2 \times 50 = 100$

First, they came to a classroom where a lonely boy sat reading. Scrooge sobbed to see his boy self, left in school over Christmas by his unloving father.

Little Fan?

We're to be together all the Christmas long.

She had a large heart!

So she had.

Next, Scrooge saw a later Christmas. His kind sister, Fan, had come to take him home. Fan was dead now, yet only today Scrooge had rebuffed Fred, her son.

I should like to be able to say a word or two to my clerk just now!

Yo ho, my boys!

Next, the Ghost took them to a merry Christmas party at the first office Scrooge had worked in. Mr Fezziwig, his employer, had been generous. A fire blazed, candles shone and there was food, a fiddler, wine and laughter. Scrooge watched and thought of poor, cold Bob Cratchit.

Spirit! ... Why do you delight to torture me?

The master-passion, Gain, engrosses you.

What then?

The scene changed again. Scrooge saw the woman he had hoped to marry. She had watched Ebenezer's love for her fade, as his passion for money grew. Sadly, she had broken their engagement.

Haunt me no longer!

Scrooge could bear no more. He seized the Ghost's hat to snuff its light out, fell into bed and slept.

The Ghost of Christmas Present

I am the Ghost of Christmas Present.

The clock struck again and Scrooge woke to see the next room ablaze with light. Shuffling to the door, he saw the walls covered with holly and the floor with food. In the middle sat a smiling giant. The Ghost rose and, holding up a horn of light, transported Scrooge out into the streets of Christmas morning.

God bless us every one!

Spirit ... tell me if Tiny Tim will live.

I see a vacant seat.

They came to the Cratchits' home. It was a bustle of Christmas preparations. Bob had just come in from church with his frail son, Tiny Tim, on his shoulders.

Hurrah!

Oh, what a wonderful pudding!

When Mrs Cratchit served a small but sizzling pudding, all the children cheered. But when Bob proposed a toast to his employer, they fell silent.

Ha, ha! Ha, ha, ha, ha! ... He said that Christmas was a humbug, as I live! ... He believed it too!

Next, they came to Fred's house. Fred was telling stories to his family of his miserly uncle. Then they all played Christmas games.

Spirit! are they yours?

They are Man's...
This boy is Ignorance.
This girl is Want.

Last, the Ghost showed Scrooge a vision: two wretched children, born of human selfishness and greed. The clock struck again. The Ghost vanished.

I am in the presence of the Ghost of Christmas Yet To Come?

I fear you more than any Spectre.

It's likely to be a very cheap funeral ... I don't know of anybody to go to it.

As it did, a silent hooded Ghost drifted like mist towards Scrooge.

It transported him to the city district where Scrooge worked.

Some businessmen Scrooge knew were laughing over a recent death.

The case of this unhappy man might be my own.

Wicked old screw ... wasn't he ...?

If he relents... Nothing is past hope.

He is past relenting... He is dead.

Am I that man?

They moved on to a dingy alley, where people were selling the same dead man's possessions for profit.

Next they saw a young family rejoicing at the man's death. They owed him money they could not pay.

"And He took a child."

Don't mind it, father.

My little, little child!

I am sure we shall none of us – forget poor Tiny Tim – shall we?

Never, father!

Scrooge felt sorry for the unmourned man. He asked the Ghost to show him the death of someone loved. The Ghost took him to the Cratchits' home. Bob had just returned from visiting a new grave, dug for Tiny Tim. The family drew close together, remembering the gentle boy they would miss so much.

No, Spirit! Oh, no, no!

EBENEZER SCROOGE

Scrooge asked the name of the friendless man. The Ghost took him to a churchyard. There, on a neglected grave, Scrooge read his own name.

Oh, tell me I may sponge away the writing on this stone!

Scrooge clutched the Ghost's hand. If he lived a better life could he prevent such a death? The hand trembled. The Ghost dissolved into a bedpost.

It was Scrooge's own bedpost. He was back in his bedroom and it was Christmas morning!

Laughing for joy, he sent a boy running to fetch a prize turkey for the Cratchits.

Then he dressed in his best and went out into the streets, filled with Christmas cheer.

Seeing one of the two gentlemen who'd come collecting for the poor, he donated a vast sum.

He stopped at his nephew's door, feeling a little shy. But he found a warm welcome and a party.

Next morning, Bob Cratchit was amazed to see warm fires in the grates and to hear of a salary rise.

From that day on, Scrooge proved the kindest, merriest old gentleman you could ever wish to meet. He was a friend to all, and to Tiny Tim – who did not die – he was a second father. When people laughed at the sudden change in him, he let them. He thanked old Marley from the bottom of his heart for the lessons he had learnt. Scrooge never saw a Ghost again, and it was always said of him that he knew how to keep Christmas well. May that be truly said of each of us – a Merry Christmas, everyone!

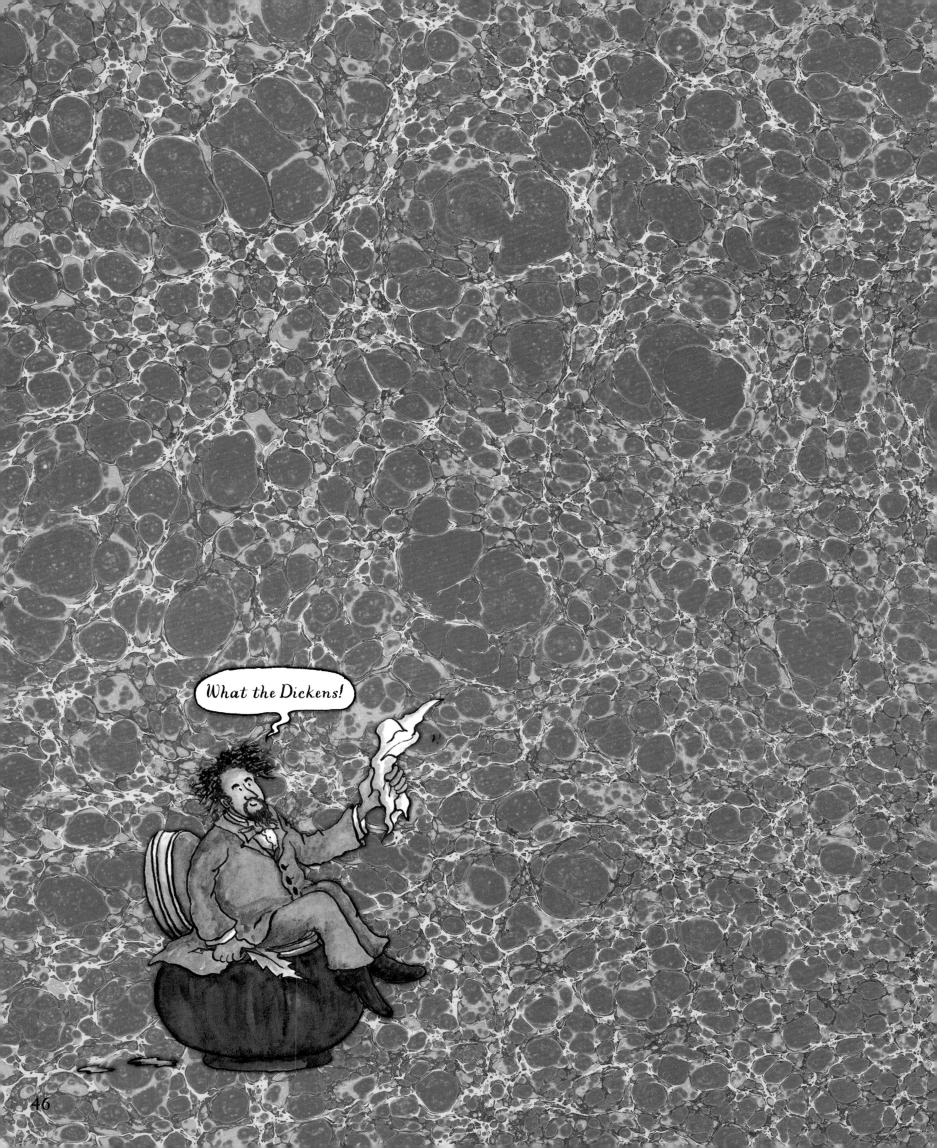

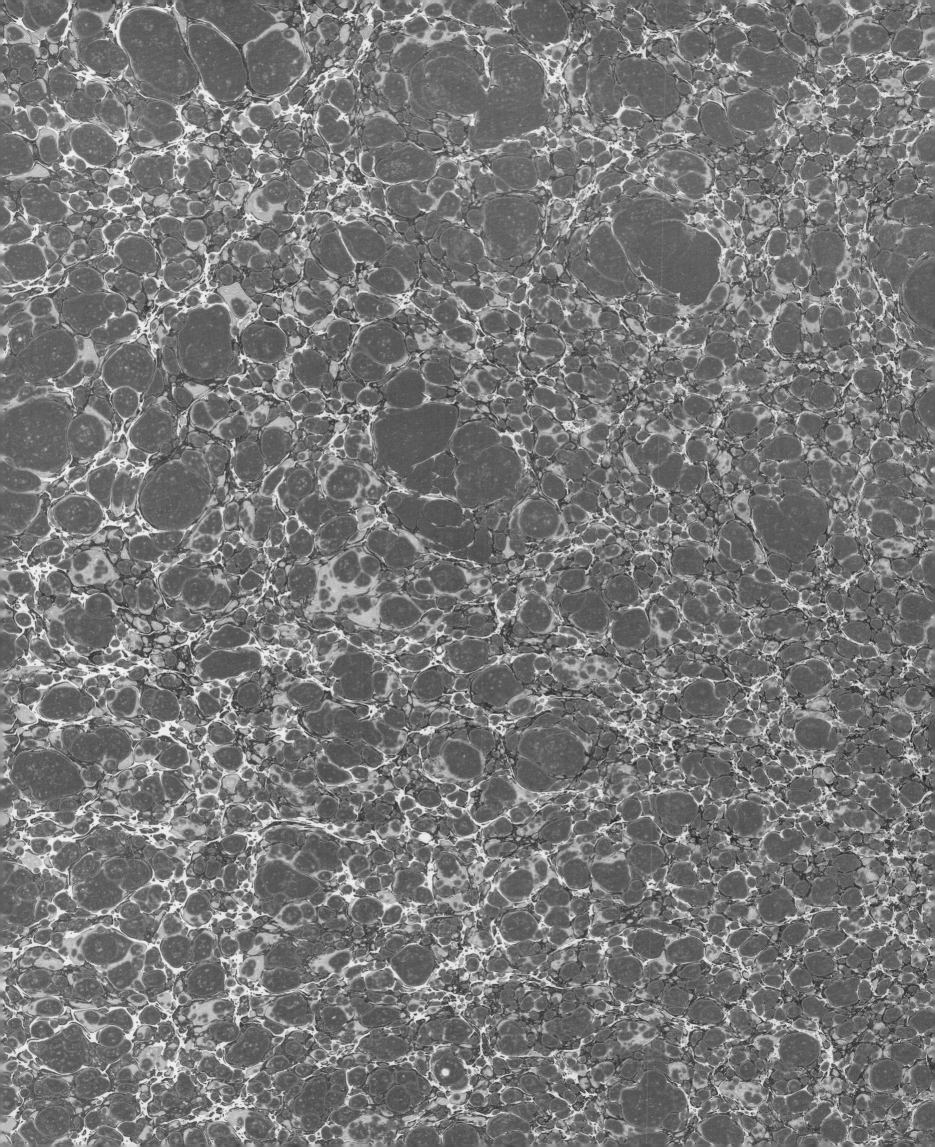